U.S.A.

Southampton Island,
Northwest Territories

Canada

St. James Bay,
Ontario

United States
of America

Central
America

Delaware Bay

Northeastern
United States

Northward path of
our Red Knot

Southward path of
our Red Knot

Range of Red Knots

French Guiana

Maranhao, Brazil

South America

San Antonio Oeste,
Argentina

Lagoa do Peixe,
Brazil

Tierra del Fuego,
Argentina/Chile

# Red Knot
## A Shorebird's Incredible Journey

## Nancy Carol Willis

## Birdsong Books
### Middletown, Delaware

February 1, Tierra del Fuego: Cool breezes brush across the southernmost tip of South America. Winter is coming. A robin-sized shorebird called a Red Knot prepares to make one of the longest animal migrations. Dark gray wing feathers replace old, worn ones. Salmon-red body feathers begin to appear.

As the departure time nears, Red Knot's heart and wing muscles grow stronger. She stuffs herself daily on tiny clams, storing excess fat to use as fuel on her journey.

February 13: Red Knot takes flight along with 100 other knots.

February 14, 900 miles north: Red Knot reaches Argentina's smooth, rocky tide pools. She swallows small mussels whole. Her gizzard grinds up the shells along with the food. Layers of fat grow thicker.

April 4, 1,000 miles farther north: Red Knot plucks snails from shallow, grassy lagoons in southern Brazil.

April 28: Red Knot flies inland over the Amazon rainforest, headed for the northeast coast of Brazil. Aided by a tailwind, she makes the 2,300-mile, nonstop flight in three days.

May 1, northeast Brazil: At low tide along the shoreline, Red Knot pulls mussels off of the tangled mangrove roots. Red breeding feathers now cover her body.

May 11: Late afternoon, Red Knot flies out over the Atlantic Ocean. With no landmarks to guide her, she makes a turn northwest toward Delaware Bay, 4,000 miles away.

May 12: At midnight, Red Knot crosses the equator. The stars and the Earth's magnetic forces help keep her on course.

May 13: Rain and wind beat against Red Knot. Her small wings pumping hard, she rises 10,000 feet above the storm to clear skies.

Exhausted, Red Knot's body fat is gone. Her body now must burn muscle for energy to keep her aloft.

May 15, Delaware Bay: As Red Knot approaches, another migration from the deep waters is ending. Horseshoe crabs by the thousands crowd the shallow shoreline. The high tide ebbs. Round horseshoe-shaped shells bump and clatter as male crabs compete for females.

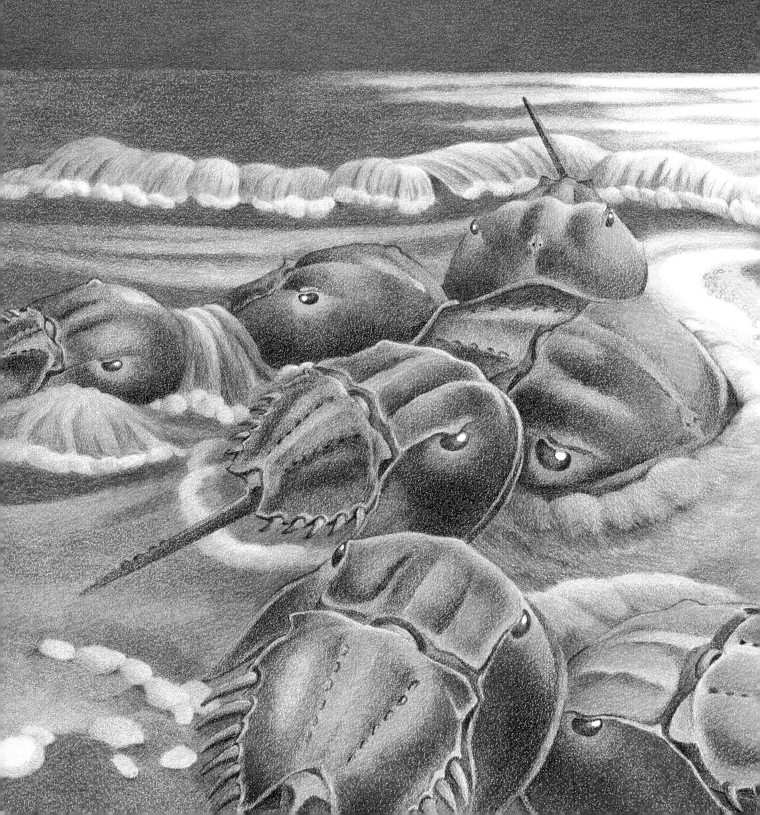

One male clasps tightly to a large female's shell as she digs a shallow nest in the sand. She lays a golf-ball-sized cluster of tiny gray-green eggs. She drags the smaller male over the eggs to fertilize them. An hour later another female accidentally digs up the nest, exposing thousands of eggs that shorebirds can now take for food.

May 15, Delaware Bay: Red Knot lands along with other knots, bone-weary and starving. Flocks of Sanderlings, sandpipers, Dunlins, and dowitchers crowd the salty shoreline. Tens of thousands of squawking shorebirds feast on the fat-rich horseshoe crab eggs.

May 18: Peck, peck, peck. Red Knot eats one horseshoe crab egg every second. If she is to double her weight in two weeks, she must eat 18,000 eggs a day! Ka-ha, ha-ha-hah, shriek the Laughing Gulls. The large black-and-white birds pester Red Knot, preventing her from eating.

All day long, motor boats roar past. Sometimes dogs chase the birds. Each time, the frightened birds burst into the air, using energy they cannot spare. Red Knot looks elsewhere for a quiet place to feed.

May 21: A flock of shorebirds forages at the high tide line. After a loud bang, a large net flies over the birds.

Red Knot is trapped underneath. Her heart beats wildly.

A huge creature grabs her, but no claws sink into her flesh. A colored flag and a metal band encircle her legs.* The creature lets go! Unharmed, Red Knot flies to safety and feeds again.

May 28: Red Knot weighs 220 grams, or eight ounces, as much as two sticks of butter. The fat fuels her next flight to the Arctic nesting grounds and gives her the energy to lay eggs. In the early evening, several thousand knots lift off. Red Knot joins them for the 1,800-mile, nonstop flight.

* Banding information may be found at the back of the book.

June 1, 10,000 miles from home: The snow banks on the Canadian tundra have begun to melt. Insects have not yet hatched, so Red Knot nibbles on seeds and scarce spiders.

June 5: Overhead a male knot calls, *Whip-poo-me, whip-poo-me.* He glides near the ground, then swoops upward again, calling, *Poo-me.*

Finally, the male
stands near Red Knot,
wings held high,
and she chooses
him as her mate.

June 8: Using his feet, the male knot digs a shallow hole into the rocky ground. He finishes the nest by lining it with dried willow leaves and soft lichens.

Red Knot lays four splotchy brown-and-green eggs in the snug nest. Together they total more than half of her weight.

June 14: A Snowy Owl swoops silently by. Red Knot freezes low on the nest until danger passes. Her speckled feathers camouflage her among the rocks and mosses.

July 3: Chicks hatch. Within hours, four downy knots snatch flies and mosquitoes to eat. Near the Arctic Circle food is now plentiful, and the sun never sets.

July 10: Red Knot departs on her southward migration, leaving her mate to protect the chicks.

July 22: The male knot leaves the Arctic, a month before his young, who can now care for themselves.

August 1: Unseen, a hungry Arctic fox approaches the young knots. He drops low to the ground. He creeps closer. He lunges. Knots scatter in all directions, diving for cover. The fox chases one bird, then another, but catches nothing!

August 3, 600 miles south: Red Knot forages along the marshy shores of James Bay. With turnstones and godwits, she devours clams and small worms that are crammed by the thousands in the mud and eelgrass.

August 6, New England coast: Recent storms have washed away the clumps of mussels along with the sand. To find food, Red Knot must fly south to the New Jersey shores.

August 25, French Guiana: Blue skies welcome Red Knot to South America. Winter is giving way to spring.

September 15, Brazil: Red Knot flies over the Amazon rainforest, the trees like a green ocean below.

October 31, Tierra del Fuego:
Red Knot touches down on
the windy coastline.

She preens a worn flight feather and then folds her wings. She tucks her bill into her back, ready for a long nap.

After nine months and 20,000 miles, Red Knot is finally home.

# Why scientists place leg bands on Red Knots

Scientists travel to distant parts of the world to study Red Knots. These places include Argentina, Brazil, Delaware Bay, and Canada. They focus their attention on the large Red Knots, because food shortages along the migration route would likely hurt them before affecting the smaller birds. After catching the birds with nets, scientists weigh and measure them. This information indicates whether the knots are healthy and fat enough to survive long distance flights. Scientists also place bands around the birds' legs that allow them to follow individual birds from year-to-year and place-to-place.

Our Red Knot wears a lime-green flag with the letters "ALX." The author chose to use those letters for her dog, Alex. She then learned that ALX is an actual Red Knot that was banded in Delaware Bay on May 14, 2004 weighing 115 grams. ALX was sighted wintering in Tierra del Fuego and again in Delaware Bay during May, 2005. Become part of an international shorebird population study by reporting shorebirds wearing leg bands to the Pan American Shorebird Program: http://www.mb.ec.gc.ca/nature/migratorybirds/pasp/index.en.html.

# Glossary

aloft (*adv.*) in the air, and especially in flight

breed (*vb.*) to produce the young of a species

camouflage (*n.*) appearance designed to conceal or hide

downy (*adj.*) soft, fluffy feathers of a young bird

ebb (*vb.*) to flow out or away

eelgrass (*n.*) a grass-like, flowering sea plant

equator (*n.*) imaginary circle around the Earth halfway between the North and South Poles

fertilize (*vb.*) create an embryo by joining the sperm of a male with the egg of a female

forage (*vb.*) to search for food

gizzard (*n.*) large, muscular part of a bird's digestive tube in which food is ground small

lagoon (*n.*) a shallow pond near or connected to a larger body of water

landmark (*n.*) object that is easy to see and can help guide the way

lichen (*n.*) a plant made up of an alga and a fungus growing together

magnetic forces (*n.*) invisible lines of electric-like power surrounding the Earth

mangrove (*n.*) a low, tropical wetlands tree with many roots above the ground

migration (*n.*) a change of locations seasonally

mussel (*n.*) a mollusk that has a long dark shell in two parts

preen (*vb.*) to smooth or clean feathers with the bill

range (*n.*) land over which animals roam, nest and feed

shorebird (*n.*) bird that lives and finds its food near shorelines, marshes, and bays

spawn (*vb.*) to produce or lay eggs

splotchy (*adj.*) covered with irregular spots

tailwind (*n.*) wind coming directly from behind

tundra (*n.*) a flat, treeless habitat near the North Pole

# A year in the life of a Red Knot

| NOV | DEC | JAN | FEB | MAR | APR | MAY | JUN | JUL | AUG | SEP | OCT | NOV | DEC |
|-----|-----|-----|-----|-----|-----|-----|-----|-----|-----|-----|-----|-----|-----|

Tierra del Fuego, Argentina & Chile

Argentina

Brazil

Delaware Bay

Canadian Arctic

James Bay, Ontario

Maritimes & Northeast U.S.

Suriname & French Guiana

Southern Brazil & Argentina

## Red Knot name and relatives

The Red Knot's common name refers to the red color of its breeding feathers and the sound of its flight note, a low "knut." Its scientific name, *Calidris canutus,* may be named for Danish King Canute. Five subspecies of Red Knots live around the world and nest in separate locations near the Arctic Circle. The *rufa* subspecies is the one depicted in this book.

Red Knots belong to a tribe of sandpipers in the Family Scolopacidae that includes Sanderling, Dunlin, Short-billed Dowitcher, and Semi-palmated Sandpiper. Other shorebirds pictured in this book include the Ruddy Turnstone, Hudsonian Godwit and Whimbrel.

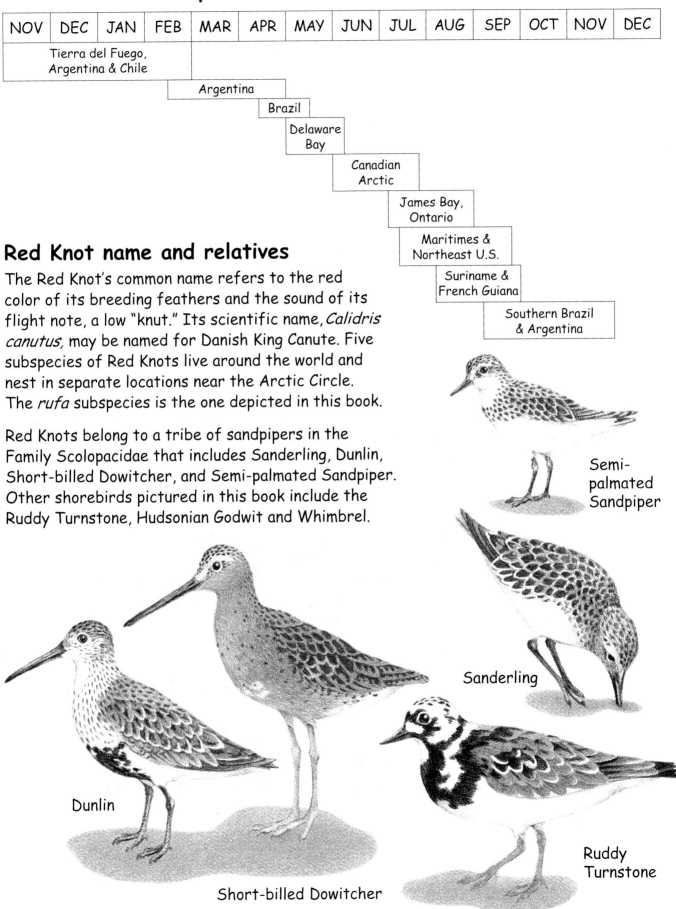

Semi-palmated Sandpiper

Sanderling

Dunlin

Short-billed Dowitcher

Ruddy Turnstone

## Why Red Knots migrate such long distances

By following the spring seasons northward, Red Knots avoid harsh winter weather. Throughout most of their range, Red Knots feed on hard-shelled mussels and clams along coastal wetlands. These habitats lack suitable nest sites and food chicks can digest. The Arctic tundra, 10,000 miles away, offers isolated nesting sites, 24 hours of daylight, and abundant insect food for chicks to eat. Female knots leave the Arctic several days after their chicks hatch. By the time the chicks are full grown, most of the males have gone, leaving the juveniles to migrate 10,000 miles with only a few adults. It is possible that only Arctic Terns migrate farther than Red Knots.

## History and conservation

Americans hunted shorebirds for food without limit for over 150 years. One account from the late 19th century describes hunters near Boston filling 60 barrels a night with six dozen knots per barrel. The birds were sold for food at market for 10 cents apiece. In 1918, Congress passed laws protecting migratory birds. But in the past 25 years, the population of *rufa* Red Knots has fallen from 200,000 to below 40,000. A team of scientists from around the world is working hard to find answers for the population crash, so that steps can be taken to help the Red Knots recover.

## Importance of Delaware Bay to Red Knot survival

Red Knots make several long-distance flights and stop to feed at only a few places along the way. Delaware Bay is the most important feeding site, because birds arrive following a 4,000-mile nonstop flight over the Atlantic Ocean. Red Knots must double their body weights before flying to the Arctic nesting grounds. The birds' ability to lay eggs and raise chicks depends on having plenty of horseshoe crab eggs to eat in Delaware Bay. But the number of horseshoe crabs laying eggs has fallen by 75 percent since 1990. For over 150 years, millions of horseshoe crabs a year were ground up for use as fertilizer or chopped up for bait in conch and eel traps. In recent years, their copper-blue blood has been used to test the purity of pharmaceutical drugs. Every year, spawning habitat is lost to housing construction and recreational use. Scientists continue to study the connection between horseshoe crabs and shorebirds.

## What's being done to help Red Knots

Saving Red Knots means protecting the places where they stop for food, and managing the food available at those places.

1986: Shores of Delaware Bay named the first International Shorebird Reserve.

1997: Protection for horseshoe crabs begins.

1998: Western Hemisphere Shorebird Reserve Network (WHRSN) identifies 34 sites in seven countries important to shorebird survival.

2001: 300-square-mile horseshoe crab sanctuary created at the mouth of Delaware Bay; limits placed on the taking of horseshoe crabs for bait.

2004: Beach collection of horseshoe crabs for bait banned during the peak shorebird season.

# Acknowledgements

The author wishes to expresses her sincere thanks to the following friends for their support of the Red Knot and this project.

Nigel A. Clark, Graham Austin, & friends: British Trust for Ornithology; Patricia M. Gonzalez: Fundacion Inalafquen; Brian A. Harrington: Manomet Center for Conservation Sciences; Allan J. Baker: Royal Ontario Museum; Michael E. Riska, Lorraine M. Fleming, & friends: Delaware Nature Society Publications Committee; Gene K. Hess, Jean L. Woods: Delaware Museum of Natural History; Gary Kreamer: Green Eggs & Sand Program; friends with the Delaware Shorebird Monitoring Program; friends with the Delaware Audubon Society; Delaware Department of Natural Resources & Environmental Control; The Premcor Refining Group; Uniqema Atlas Pointe Site, Maggie Alexander, Kerry Lowe, Karen D. Quinn: elementary school teachers & librarians; Lynda Graham-Barber: writer & friend; Karen Murphy: friend.

## for Jude and Madison,

## Red Knot: A Shorebird's Incredible Journey

Summary: Describes the 20,000-mile annual migration of a shorebird called a Red Knot, from the tip of South America to the Arctic tundra nesting grounds and back.

Library of Congress Control Number 2005904707
Cloth: ISBN 10: 0966276140, ISBN 13: 9780966276145
Paper: ISBN 10: 0966276159, ISBN 13: 9780966276152

Published in the United States by Birdsong Books
Printed in China